COMPOUNDING YOUR CONFIDENCE

Strategies to Expand Your Opportunities for SUCCESS

Jill J. Johnson, MBA

Other books by Jill J. Johnson:

From the BOLD Questions Series:

BOLD Questions – Business Strategy Edition

BOLD Questions – Opportunities Edition

BOLD Questions – Leadership Edition

BOLD Questions – Decision Making Edition

Enduring Entrepreneurs (coming soon)

Learn more about Jill online and check out
her free white papers at

www.jcs-usa.com

COMPOUNDING YOUR CONFIDENCE

Strategies to Expand Your Opportunities for SUCCESS

Jill J. Johnson, MBA

Compounding Your Confidence

Copyright © 2018 Jill J. Johnson

Published by Johnson Consulting Services
Minneapolis, Minnesota
www.jcs-usa.com

Limit of liability/disclaimer of warranty:
While the publisher and author have used their best efforts in preparing this book, they make no representations or warranties with respect to the accuracy or completeness of the contents of this book and specifically disclaim any implied warranties of merchantability or fitness for a particular purpose. The advice and strategies contained herein may not be suitable for your situation. This work is sold on the understanding that the publisher and author are not engaged in rendering professional services. Neither the publisher or author shall be liable for damages arising herefrom. If professional advice or other expert assistance is required, the services of a competent professional should be sought.

Book Edited by Connie Anderson, Words & Deeds, Inc. www.wordsanddeedsinc.com

Book Design by Chris Mendoza, CAMM. arts LLC. www.chrisdmendoza.com

For information on Jill or on how to order bulk copies of this book,
or the BOLD Questions series, contact her at: www.jcs-usa.com

ISBN 978-0-9984236-4-7

1. **Business 2. Self-Help 3. Non-Fiction**

Printed in the United States of America

Author's Note

This is a work of creative nonfiction. The events are portrayed to the best of my memory. While all the stories in this book are true, some names and identifying details have been changed to protect the privacy of the people involved. The conversations in the book all come from my recollections.

This book is dedicated to my coaches

You have challenged me to plant my feet firmly on the ground and then reach for the stars. You demanded excellence from me. You taught me how to navigate the road to success. Without you, none of this would ever have been possible.

Contents

Introduction

Confidence is an elusive characteristic for many of us as we journey through life and our careers. Doubt, low self-esteem, and a lack of emotional control undermine our ability to deal with adversity or failure. Most people believe that you are born with confidence—either you have it, or you don't. This self-limiting belief is why so many people hold themselves back from ever reaching their true potential. Confidence is a significant life skill. Developing it is an essential core competency that's necessary to achieve any level of success.

What if there was a way for you to build your confidence? What if you could learn how to believe in yourself so you could leverage all your skills and talents to make a difference in your community or become a leader within your organization?

There is a way. You must take responsibility for building your own confidence. It cannot be delegated to others. You don't need to take big risks or make huge leaps. It is the cumulative impact of small and focused efforts to build your skills that will increase your confidence over time. As your confidence compounds, you will find you can accomplish vastly more than you ever dreamed was possible. Confidence allows you to have impact far beyond your job title or position.

Building your confidence requires a disciplined focus on boldly seeking out and accepting new opportunities as you reach for higher rungs of success. Maintaining your confidence requires the ability to coalesce your experience with the ability to trust yourself. There are three fundamental keys to developing your confidence:

1. Progressions
2. Practice
3. Presentation

My goal in writing this book is to provide you with the takeaways you need to compound your confidence. I want to give you the last little boost you need to be able to accept the risk, challenge or leadership role you are about to face. You must be getting ready to take a step outside of your comfort zone or you would not be reading this now. No matter your experience level or age, confidence can be a challenge. It is important to understand we all need a boost now and then.

The best way to show you how to compound your confidence is to share my story. By sharing with you how I have navigated building my career, business, and leadership skills, you will learn how you can expand your own confidence to build a better life for yourself.

While my story tells the arc of my successes, I have also learned hard lessons and have made many mistakes along the way. Not life-threatening or career-ending mistakes, but these mistakes tested my confidence. I had confidence roadblocks I needed to find a way around too. Each of these challenges forced me to try different approaches until I found out what worked best for me. I learned different strategies to expand my opportunities for success by learning from every experience. You can do the same.

Chapter 1

Finding Your Golden Egg

I won a pony when I was three years old, not because my name was pulled out in a drawing. I had to act. I sat in the backseat of our car, arguing with my older brother. Jeff was in the front seat, and we were yelling at each other while our mother drove us to the park for our hometown Easter egg hunt.

I kept repeating with giddy enthusiasm, "I'm going to find the golden egg. I'm going to find the golden egg."

Jeff dismissed me, saying, "That will never happen."

We continued to bicker all the way to the park. Despite Jeff's badgering, I was convinced I would find the golden egg.

Once we arrived, a large crowd of children and their parents were roaming around waiting for the event to start. I don't remember what the signal was for the hunt to begin, but suddenly we were all running in different directions. I ran wildly to gather up lots of the candy that had been spread out all over the ground.

I held tightly onto my little wicker basket as I stooped to pick up the candies and chocolate Easter bunnies.

After I gathered a basket full of candy, I turned to my mother and announced with a clear and determined voice, "I'm going to go get the golden egg now, Mommy."

Her response was classic, as only a busy mom struggling to keep an eye on two children of vastly different ages in a crowd could say, "OK, Honey."

In an instant, I bolted from her and ran directly over to the big slide where I picked up the golden egg. I ran right to it. It was the first time I ever darted away from my mother. I ran with confidence. I don't know how I knew the egg was there. I simply knew running to the ladder of the big slide was the right thing to do. I trusted myself, and I ran to pick up my prize.

Finding the golden egg meant I won the grand prize of the whole Easter egg hunt—a Shetland pony. Not a giant stuffed pony, but a real one.

I have a vivid memory of my dad having to come up to the park to get us. We had no saddle or bridle. He found an old piece of rope and lifted me onto the back of the pony. We walked down the hill to my grandparents' home where we were living at the time. I cannot remember exactly what my dad muttered as we guided my pony to his new home, but I know it was a lot of cuss words.

Dad was right to cuss because the pony I named Goldie was the meanest pony God ever created. It is also probably why the farmer donated him to the Easter egg hunt in the first place.

Winning this Shetland pony was my first golden moment of being confident. It was about relying on myself, trusting I was traveling in the right direction, and acting on my own initiative.

I did not grow up with a silver spoon. My father owned an auto body repair shop in Hudson, Wisconsin. At the time, Hudson was a small river town of around 5,000 people located just across the border from our neighboring state of Minnesota.

My dad was the classic entrepreneur and I never saw him with clean hands until we buried him. My mom was the savvy business brain. To make ends meet and ensure our family had a stable income, in the early days of the business, she worked as an executive secretary at the nearby world headquarters of 3M.

Each of my parents gave me special insights, both easy and hard, providing me with a foundation for learning how to build my confidence. While they both lacked much formal education, they demonstrated the importance of on-going learning as they ran our small family business. My parents taught me much of what I know about customer service and delivering quality work.

My mom constantly pushed my confidence. She insisted I have big dreams for my life. However, I had no idea how you go from being a small-town kid with blue-collar parents to becoming something more. Heck, I had no idea what something more even was or could be. One thing was clear; I would have to figure this out myself.

When I was a child, I was known around town as Bobby Johnson's little girl. How did I go from the local auto body repair shop owner's daughter to being congratulated for winning a national award by the President of the United States at the White House? How did I develop enough confidence as a management consultant to be able to impact billions of dollars worth of business decisions for my clients? How did I develop the ability to stand on a stage and hold the attention of thousands of people in the audience? How did I develop enough professional savvy to be inducted into two business Halls of Fame? Those are big arcs for anyone. How does such a big transition happen, especially to someone like me who comes from such a modest background? I am not sharing this with you to brag, but to provide you with clarity that anything is possible for you too. I had to navigate confusion and uncertainty at each stage of my personal growth. You can too.

The key was finding ways to build my confidence to allow me to move from one level of success to the next. I discovered you must take calculated risks so you can make these moves. You must be willing to learn.

To prove to yourself you truly have it, your confidence must be tested. It is easy to be confident when you are in the safety of your own home, or when you are surrounded by family or loyal friends who love you. You can be confident of your ability to pay your bills even if you are working in a job you don't love because you have the security of a steady paycheck. When the safety net is gone is the time when your confidence will be tested.

I built my confidence over a long period of time. It was step by step. I made some missteps too. Some experiences were embarrassing failures. Still I managed to leverage one experience into another and I learned something from all of them. As I navigated my career and the complexities of adult life, I grew more confident in my abilities to handle myself in difficult situations. What I learned along the path of my success provided me with the self-assurance to even speak with confidence to the then-leader of the free world.

Many people want to achieve success or become recognized as a leader. Unfortunately, for most this is only a wish. Few are willing to consistently work to build the skills necessary to attain success or be recognized as an effective leader. They are unwilling to be open to learning new ideas or take on new challenges.

Confidence is the essential ingredient differentiating those who get access to leadership opportunities. I have been in the boardrooms, the back rooms, and the executive suites with Fortune 100 presidents and CEOs, as well as with board members from Fortune 500 companies. I have been with some extraordinary entrepreneurs who built incredible businesses. I have worked with leaders of significant non-profit organizations making a difference in their community. *I know from experience: their confidence propels them into these rooms. Their confidence in themselves is also what keeps them there.*

Many studies say people who are perceived to be leaders are tall, attractive, and male. I am short and female. I can never walk into a room and "own it" simply because I'm the tallest one in the room. Nor am I a glamorous supermodel. I need to use other tactics to establish my credentials for being invited into these rooms. I also need to maintain my confidence to be effective in them.

In this book, I will pull back the curtain to share how I approach building my confidence. I always keep in mind, ever since David slew Goliath—the little person can win. It's all about having confidence and applying the right approach to winning.

The arc from being the little girl who won the Shetland pony to the woman I am today required the deliberate development of a success strategy. I have intentionally built my skills so I can execute them with confidence. My success strategy is still always active and always evolving.

I began building my formal confidence strategy when I was in college. In one of my business classes, our professor discussed the importance of evaluating the strengths, weaknesses, opportunities, and threats when engaging in business planning for a company. He called it a SWOT Analysis using the first initials of each word.

The SWOT Analysis concept intrigued me. I was inspired and could see another use for this concept. I decided to do a full-blown SWOT Analysis using myself as the target of the evaluation. I was nearing graduation and viewed this approach as an opportunity for me to evaluate my *personal* strengths, weaknesses, opportunities, and threats. I hoped the insights I gained would assist me in developing my plan for finding the right job to start my professional career.

As I created my plan, I focused on the smallest details. I carefully conducted a market evaluation by looking at whom I was going to be competing against for these future jobs. I developed tactics to achieve my future job goal. The exercise of thinking through my plan in such detail provided me with many opportunities to identify what I already could do, and clarified where I needed to grow. This exercise also removed the fear I felt about taking this next step toward my future. Removing the emotion of being afraid to find a job allowed me to more objectively assess my situation and identify what I could leverage to get a foot in the door.

Okay, I will admit I was a unique 22-year-old. My plan included an assessment on everything it would take to get a job. I considered what business suits I was going to wear. Suits were the "packaging" of the product that I was. I was a young woman pursuing a Master's degree in Business Administration (MBA) at a time when most women did not go into the corporate world in professional roles. I needed to dress the part to fit in. I needed a well-written resume to serve as my marketing brochure. I considered my "price" because my salary would be the number I was going to ask for when, *not if,* I received a job offer. Next, I developed the plan to build my skills for the areas I had identified as my weaknesses. I also thought about how I would "sell" myself in the interviews by leveraging my skills and experience.

This plan ultimately became more than a personal business plan. As I look back on it now, it became my Confidence Plan. Consistently enhancing my Confidence Plan is a huge part of how I travel through my life. Working on building my confidence is what brought me from being the daughter of a blue-collar entrepreneur to the success I have achieved so far.

I continue to refine my Confidence Plan. I work on my confidence each day because I still test myself and strive for even more. I am always learning. Of course, this approach to life often creates moments of self-doubt until I master a new skill or new level of achievement.

I am going to break it down to show how you too can create your own Confidence Plan. You *can* develop your own plan to enhance your confidence. You *can* think through the actions and steps you will take to achieve your success.

Of course, there is more to the story. Building my confidence and achieving success did not happen overnight. It took more than developing my plan; it also required the confidence to act on it.

Chapter 2

What Do You Want?

At the age of eighteen, I decided I wanted to become a management consultant. In the late 1970s, girls didn't go to college to major in business, mainly because it was almost impossible at that time to get accepted into these academic degree tracks. Despite this, I was determined to get into a high-quality collegiate business program.

Frankly, thinking I could become a management consultant was a ridiculous and audacious idea. In this era, management consultants were rare. Today everyone calls themselves a consultant, whether they are a hairdresser or a contract laborer. Back then, only those with exceptional business skills and a strong business mind could enter the consulting profession—made up almost exclusively of older men who were much more seasoned in business.

In high school, my mom made me get involved in the Junior Achievement (JA) program. At that time, JA operated differently than what is offered today. We set up small businesses and worked in them every week. Each company created and sold a product.

My company made candles and sold a cookbook we had created. We also had key functional roles as we ran our little companies ranging from sales to overseeing quality control. My senior year, I was our company president.

JA held a major national conference every summer in Bloomington, Indiana. The conference was called the National Junior Achievement Conference (NAJAC). Only the top Achievers out of the more than 300,000 high school students involved in the program went to NAJAC. One of the most exciting parts of the conference was the competition for Achievers who had won the award for their functional role at the local level. Winners received scholarships, and I needed scholarships to pay for my college education.

To have a shot at winning a scholarship, I understood I needed to invest time to get ready to compete effectively at the national level. Winning the local President of the Year contest had been hard. It would be even more challenging to be a contender nationally for the NAJAC President of the Year competition. I spent my entire summer preparing for the big week in August. I analyzed *Harvard Business Review* case studies. I toured the Federal Reserve Bank to learn how they inject money into the economy. I interviewed successful local entrepreneurs and business executives to learn about their business strategies.

Out of the blue, I received a phone call from Tony, with whom I had co-chaired a big regional JA conference earlier that year. He had a proposition to support my preparation. He advised, "Jill, you need to get down to Chicago. I have set up a meeting with a business executive I met on a train. I know this meeting will help you prepare for the NAJAC competition."

After I talked with Tony, I knew with certainty I needed to be at this meeting. I found my mother working on a crossword puzzle in our living room. I informed her with the same determined voice I had used when I found the golden egg, "Mom, I have a business meeting in Chicago next week. It will help me prepare for NAJAC. I need to go."

I was barely out of high school, but to her everlasting credit, my mother had the confidence in me to let me go to this meeting that ultimately changed my life.

After arriving from my long drive, Tony and I went to our lunch meeting at the Union League Club, an old private club in downtown Chicago. There I met Robert Cardinal. He was a successful management consultant. I had never heard of this profession. During our lunch, he talked about what he did as a consultant. He described his work with clients, the impact he made, and the traveling he did. I was mesmerized. In an instant, I had full clarity this career was to be my future profession. I walked out of the meeting knowing, "This is what I am going to be."

I had no idea how I would make this happen. Nor was there anyone in my life at the time that knew the path needed to make this happen for a young woman from a small town. Having a big dream was not going to be enough. How was I going to pull off this one? I had confidence I could find a way to do this. *I had to.*

Several years later, I was sitting in a classroom listening to a guest speaker at Drake University in Des Moines, Iowa, where I was attending college. It was highly unusual for our professors to allow someone from outside academia to speak to any class. The speaker was a prominent Drake alum who was there to talk with the business students. He was Joe Batten, the founder of an international management consulting firm based in Des Moines. His clients included world-class companies such as McDonald's, Xerox, Marriott, and IBM.

To say Joe Batten was a big fish would be an understatement. He was one of America's leading management consultants. At the time, his firm was one of the best-known human resource development companies in the country. Joe's friends and peers included Zig Ziglar and Og Mandino. It was like being in a room today with John Maxwell, Jim Collins or Brian Tracy. Joe had written a classic business bestseller with more than one million copies in print. He was considered an icon in the management consulting world.

I decided I needed to meet him. I waited in line after his speech to ask Joe for his business card, which I tucked carefully into my backpack. I had no idea when I would reach out to him, but I knew I eventually would. I had taken the first step: I made a connection. Joe would not remember me; however, I knew he would remember he had spoken to the students at Drake.

After I completed my MBA, it was time to reach out to Joe. I networked with other professionals to get them to mention my name to him as well as to key members of his consulting team. Soon I had my shot–I had scheduled a meeting.

My bold request for a meeting turned into an interview with Joe's firm, and it resulted in a job offer. I ended up becoming the first woman in Joe's company history to be hired as a consultant in the management consulting division of their business. They had hired women before who were trainers in their education division, but none had ever cracked the code to be hired in the management consulting side of the practice. Until me.

When you look at how you are connecting with people today, is there somebody you want to meet who can help your career? Or someone you would like to interview to learn more about how they achieved their success? I bet you can think of more than one person. What bold action can you take to make the connection? How can you prepare to maximize the time you have with them?

Have confidence.
Take a chance.
Take the responsibility
to ask for what you want.
You might just get it.

I am vastly more confident about life and my ability to handle a difficult situation today than I was at twenty-two because confidence compounds over time. As you gain experience, you will gain confidence.

Confidence building is a life's journey. Your confidence will compound exponentially if you act each day to support it. This means you are continually implementing and re-defining your Confidence Plan as you move through your life. Each stage of your personal growth requires a new foundation of confidence to ensure success. The foundation for your confidence is built by your daily choices and the effort you make.

As I noted earlier, it takes three keys to building your confidence: progressions, practice, and presentation. Each provides you with the foundation necessary to move forward with confidence. They also offer the insight you will need to regroup when your confidence fails. Now it is time to think deeply about what you can do to build your confidence using these essential keys to your success.

Keep in mind confidence is a skill. As with any new skill, you must practice it over and over for it to become something you can do with ease.

The first step is to identify the skill you need to develop in order to move toward whatever your next level of success is.

- Do you need to improve a skill you are already good at?

- Do you need to learn something new?

- What skills must you practice so you can flawlessly deliver under pressure?

- From which teachers do you need to learn?

By answering these questions, you will be able to start identifying the resources you need. As you improve your skills, you will become more confident. Then you will start to project your well-earned confidence to others.

When you have confidence in your skills, you are building confidence in yourself.

Chapter 3

Build Your Confidence Through Progressions

As a child, I would walk down to the river near our home with my devoted Springer Spaniel dog. Teddy would guard me while I sat along the banks of the Willow River and dreamed about my future. As I dreamed, I watched the flow of the water. I realized when water hits an obstacle, it simply moves around it or wears it down so it can freely pass. The water's success in moving forward is about the flow. It is about the movement. It is about the action.

Watching the water provided me with insight about what I needed to do with own my future. I couldn't rely on anyone else to make it happen for me, especially once I decided to become a management consultant. Becoming a management consultant was such a big dream. It was highly unrealistic given my gender, age, and lack of social connections. I had no one in my life who could open doors for me to such a prestigious occupation. I had to find my own path to achieve my goal. I had to hack the trail myself to build the path, and I had to be brave enough to walk it alone.

Was I terrified? Absolutely.

Did I think I might fail? Yes, I did, every damn day.

Life is about moving forward. It's about finding the inner courage deep within you to find a way to achieve your goals, despite your fear, so you can create the life you desire.

Desire is not enough. You must make it happen. It is not going to be gifted to you or handed out on a silver platter. You must find your way. Confidence, or the lack of it, will be your constant companion as you move toward achieving your goals.

Start looking at your efforts as progressions. Progressions are continuously layering your skills over time to develop deeper levels of refinement. As you refine your skills, you progress from one level of success to the next. Over time, your progressions become your confidence foundation.

I was a competitive gymnast in high school. Once our season was over, I continued to train five days a week at a private gymnastics club. My mother would pick me up at 3:05 p.m. after school got out and drive me to the gym.

While she drove, I sat in the back seat of our Volkswagen Bug. I ate the cold dinner she had prepared for me. When I was done, I put on my gymnastics leotard and crawled into the front seat. I would practice my clarinet or work on my homework while we drove 45 minutes to the training center where I took lessons. I'd train with the coaches until 9:00 every evening, and would finish my homework in the car on the way home, often by flashlight.

We had to travel nearly 80 miles round trip every day because I attended the top training center in the region. I had access to the best coaches who could help me learn the skills I needed to become the best gymnast I could be. They had trained girls who were competing on the U.S. National Team at the elite level. These coaches knew what it took to get results. They expected a lot out of their young gymnasts. I thrived in the demanding environment.

Their constant feedback told us what we were doing wrong and what we needed to improve. The criticism was never-ending. Point your toes. Straighten your legs. Push higher. Land steady. Try again. Everything we did in our practice was designed to provide us with the confidence we needed to receive higher scores when we were actually competing in gymnastics meets. Practice was only the preparation for the competition. Our coaches made the practices count. They used these practices to build both our physical and mental foundation for competing successfully. They were also building our confidence.

Don't be afraid of criticism if the advice is intended to help you become better so you perform with greater precision and skill.

While feedback and criticism sting, it is what helps you progress. As you do better, you gain confidence, and a good coach will then find something else for you to improve. You must develop the on-going habit of continually trying to enhance your skills. If you shut out guidance to help you improve, you will stagnate, and your growth will stop.

Why did I train so much with such a high level of discipline? Why did I listen to all the constant criticism and feedback? I wanted to be the best gymnast I could become.

The same thing holds true for you. What do you want to become better at?

To become exceptionally good at any skill, you must master it. How do you master a skill? By learning it through incremental progressions. It is easier to focus your efforts if you break it down into smaller components so you can understand how to improve each aspect of the skill.

In gymnastics, everything is about risk management. To manage the risks as you learn a new skill, you make incremental progressions.

For example, once you learn how to do a good cartwheel on the floor, you prepare to do it on a balance beam. The next step of the progression is to work on your cartwheel on a line on the floor. As you master this, you upgrade to doing your cartwheel on a small balance beam positioned on the floor. By adding this new element simulating the top of balance beam, you learn how to place your hands properly. You also begin to understand how to move your body through the cartwheel to land on a four-inch-wide piece of equipment. You are protected from major injury because it has no height. Even if you fall, you are not going to get seriously hurt.

Once you master the floor beam, you practice your cartwheel on a balance beam now raised one-foot off the floor. After mastering this low level, you learn to do your cartwheel on the four-foot-high beam like the ones you see on television in the Olympics.

Then you start all over again and learn how to do a cartwheel without your hands. You go through the same sequence of learning your skill progression.

I was never "the best" gymnast. I trained with girls who were dreaming of going to the Olympics. Those ten- and thirteen-year olds could flip and twist twenty times better than I could. They were fearless. I started gymnastics later in life. I was a geriatric gymnast when I began training seriously at the age of 12. I was already old enough to understand how badly you could get hurt if you messed up a trick. Trust me, it affects your perspective.

Yet the most important lesson I learned from my gymnastics training was to approach my life and career by taking calculated risks. You can too. This is how you minimize your potential for injury resulting from a failure in executing a skill. You can minimize the injury to both your body and your ego. You move through learning your new skills by using progressions. This means allowing others to give you feedback so you can focus your efforts on the critical elements necessary to improve your performance. You also need to learn how to give feedback to yourself to improve without relying on others to do it for you. You will go through this same sequence with every new skill.

No matter what you do, whether you are practicing a full twisting back flip or learning to give a speech, every skill is learned based on progressions. With each progression, you learn to overcome your fear. As you lose your fear, you gain more confidence in your ability. You develop the sense memory to trust yourself. As you trust yourself, you gain more confidence. Then you can address the finer details of the skill to increase your finesse.

As you develop confidence, it starts to show in your performance. As it shows in your performance, you move to a whole new level of ability and mastery. Confidence results in awards, promotions, new opportunities, and greater success. What are the progressions for the skills you need to work on next?

As I improved as a gymnast, I set a personal goal to go to the State gymnastics tournament. I came close in my junior year in high school, but I fell off the balance beam at the last qualifying meet for State. I was disappointed in myself because the fall was the result of a dumb thing. I did not need a coach to tell me what had happened, I knew. I lost my focus and fell on an easy skill. I missed my chance.

I was determined to achieve my goal the next year. I dedicated my summer to working out even harder at the gym, going seven days a week. I trained with a vengeance. I even had a small balance beam in our living room so I could practice at home. My dad made it out of two-by-fours and stapled a piece of carpet over the top of it to cover the nails. I was constantly stretching, dancing, and visualizing reaching my goal to go to State. I did pull-ups, sit-ups, and I ran every day at training. I grew stronger and more confident in my skills.

Unfortunately, life intervened in the most unexpected way. Prior to the end of my junior year in high school, one of my teachers noticed a large tumor on my throat. In between working out at the gym, I saw several doctors who concluded I needed to have major surgery as they thought I had cancer. Fortunately, I did not, but after the surgery, my physical strength was gone. I lost the results of all my efforts over the summer months to prepare my body to achieve my goal.

As I was healing from the surgery, I could not let go of my goal. I was still determined to go to State. I went back to the beginning. I started with my mindset. I wrote a note to myself and stuck it on my bathroom mirror. I put notes in my schoolbooks and in my wallet. I hid notes everywhere. They were reminders to myself.

The phrase I wrote was: *"I can, I will, I am, and I'm going to."* To me this meant:

I can execute the skills I am still able to do with precision.

I will do the work required to rebuild my strength.

I am going to be successful in my competitions during the season.

And I'm going to qualify go to State.

I repeated this mantra to myself over and over. *"I can, I will, I am, and I'm going to."*

I said my mantra out loud while I was driving my car. I whispered it into the bathroom mirror. I probably even muttered it while I was sleeping and dreaming about my future.

With each use of this mantra, I was conditioning my mindset for success. Each time I verbalized it, I believed with more certainty I could achieve it. Repeating my mantra kept me focused so I took the necessary actions each day to move me closer to my goal.

I still use mantras when I need to remind myself of my own possibilities. It helps me to clarify the actions I need to take to continue moving toward achieving my latest goal. What are the mantras you need to say to yourself to move you closer to achieving your goals?

I used progressions to go back to the basics of my training to build my strength to regain what I had physically lost after the surgery. I used my mantra to train my mind and fight my way back to believe I could still compete. This mantra supported me through the hard work of starting all over again with my training.

I never regained everything I had lost physically. Yet what I could still do, I did exceptionally well. I could no longer safely execute my back handspring on the balance beam (at that time, this was a very advanced skill), but I could do my routines with precise form, superb technique, and exceptional style. Straight legs. Toes always pointed. Higher amplitude on my skills. Arm movements demonstrating grace. Shoulders held with confidence as I stood ready to begin my routine. I was going to pick up points for my score by incorporating the skill refinement I developed by integrating all the feedback into my execution.

I can, I will, I am, and I'm going to.

It worked. I became the first girl from Hudson to qualify for the Wisconsin state high school gymnastics competition. At the State gymnastics meet, I learned one of the most valuable lessons of my life. I had set my goal *too low*. I realized my goal was only to get there in order to compete. *My goal should have been to win.*

I had a momentary lapse of concentration and fell off the beam during the competition. I was out. As I watched the other girls competing in the State finals later that night, I realized if I had been more focused on having a bigger goal, I would have achieved more. Even with all I had lost after my surgery, I was good enough to have been in the finals. I was good enough to have been a contender to place in the State finals.

Unfortunately, my knowledge about my competition through-out Wisconsin had been too minimal. As a result, I never under-stood what the real potential for my success at State could have been. I did not bring everything I was capable of to compete in my event. I had not believed I could compete to win. I was too focused on just "participating" in the meet.

Had I fully understood the possibilities of my potential and believed with all my heart, I would have prepared for my competition with more confidence. I would have competed more effectively and I would have had a greater outcome. I would have also tried harder to stay on the balance beam.

This is what you need to do in your career and in your life. You need to figure out what calculated risks you can take so you can find a way to move yourself forward to your dreams and goals. As you know by now, confidence compounds.

What progressions can you make to move yourself forward? What do you need to know and understand about the others you are competing with to give you the confidence you need so you can be a contender? Figure it out.

Next, set your goal a level higher than you think you can achieve. Don't be your own glass ceiling.

I read a lot of biographies about famous and successful people. One common theme in all of them is the most transformative figures of history all had doubts. They wondered if they were doing the right thing. They feared nothing they did was ever going to matter. They were often afraid they would fail.

By reading book after book, it became clear to me that these extraordinary people took action to compound their confidence. They honed their skills through their successes, mistakes, and failures. They learned from their experiences and focused on how they could do better next time. With each successive effort, they engaged in building skill progressions that ultimately resulted in their attainment of their historic success or in changing the world.

Often their feats went far beyond anything they had ever imagined.

The life stories of all the transformative and amazing people in history follow these same lines: *I will prepare and someday my chance will come. I will be confident in my abilities to make a difference when it does.* And they did.

You can too.

Chapter 4

Building Your Confidence Requires Practice

You know the saying, "Luck is what happens when preparation meets opportunity." It is so true. If you're not prepared, you won't have any confidence in yourself when the opportunity to move forward toward your dreams presents itself.

You must always be preparing so you have developed your skills *before* you need them. To be prepared to progress to a level beyond where you are now, you need to look ahead. Pay attention to what others at that level are doing. Ask yourself, "What else is going to be needed from me as I move up to my next level of success?"

This is what I mean by progression. Start thinking. Start acting. Work on your skills in small bites. You can practice your skill development anywhere—at home, at school, in your job, in a church group. You can even practice while you are interacting with your children, shopping at the grocery store or coaching soccer. Anywhere.

Finding opportunities to practice new skills are all around you.

You should plan to practice your new skills both inside and outside of work. Here are a few ways you can begin your practice.

- *Volunteer for It:* Find assignments that expose you to more people and can augment your experience. By volunteering to participate, you will gain many opportunities to practice your skills.

- *Agree to Do It:* If someone you respect asks you to take on an assignment or join a committee, say "Yes." Then perform your assignment with exceptional quality and reliability.

- *Ask for It:* Tell people what you want to work on next. Don't wait for them to figure it out. Ask others to help you find opportunities to practice your evolving skills. Be specific.

- *Apply for It:* Whether it is a board position, your next job or an award, put your hat in the ring. Put a plan in motion to develop your credentials ahead of time so you are a compelling option worthy of consideration. Be sure you submit a well-thought out and strong application.

- *Say It Out Loud:* Practice saying your key messages in front of others before you ever need to say them when it counts. Practice mock job interviews with friends so you can learn to talk about what you offer before you are immersed in the stress of an interview.

I was twenty-five when I began serving on my first board of directors for a small non-profit professional organization. It wasn't the most impressive board I have ever served on; however, it was the most important board that impacted my early leadership development—because it was my first. The leaders of the organization saw my potential and asked me to join them in taking on some additional responsibility.

You're probably thinking you are too busy to serve on a board or volunteer for a committee leadership role. I hear this all the time. This is taking a very narrow viewpoint and limits your opportunities.

Volunteer leadership experience can have an exceptional impact on your entire career.

By agreeing to serve in any leadership role, you will have an opportunity to practice your new skills. Volunteer roles are essential to minimizing the risks of your practice. Confidence will come to you faster when you practice in a lower risk environment such as volunteering with an association. The ultimate stakes will not be as high there as if you are only practicing the skill in your day job. This also means you will progress at a much more rapid pace.

A perfect example of this is my young mentee, Kathleen. She has a vision for what she wants in her career and is willing to act to make progress. Kathleen invests in herself. She took a night class at a local college to obtain additional education on a key skill she wanted to build for her future. Her investment in a single night class enabled her to take an exam to certify her knowledge. When she passed the exam, she earned a professional certification for the skill. This built her confidence and gave her the professional credential to prove she had the skill. She spoke up at her firm and volunteered to handle a special project. The role was very high profile, and the stakes for the outcome were important to the company. While this role was not yet her full-time job, she began building the foundational skills for her resume so she could expand on them in the future. Kathleen volunteered and stepped up. She prepared for the skill and used the basics of what she learned to successfully manage the project. She evaluated what she did well and what she vowed to improve on the next time. She understood she needed to build her skills using progressions. Today this skill is a key part of her role as a manager.

Your confidence will compound if you volunteer because you will have multiple opportunities to develop your expertise. This can lead to working with different generations. You can learn from people who are both older and younger than you. You will expand your network of contacts too. You can practice some element of a skill you will need to prepare for your next promotion. You can even use a volunteer role to practice speaking up with confidence. Whatever you need to practice, you can do this when you volunteer.

With practice, you will build deeper awareness of yourself. You will develop greater confidence. You will demonstrate your emerging growth in mastering your new skill. This is one of the best professional outcomes of volunteering. This practice will prepare you for your next level of success.

If someone you respect reaches out to ask you to volunteer for a new role, do it. They obviously see value in you that is worth tapping. You become your own worst enemy to achieving success if you say "No."

Getting the opportunity is one thing; what do you do with it when you get it is even more important. Practicing your new skills consistently builds your confidence. Practice is essential before you can rely on it. You need your new skill to be fully integrated with your confidence so you can rely on using it. It becomes a part of you. It is essential to intentionally practice your new skills. Keep practicing so you can progress to the next stage of your skill building.

Remember to consistently deliver your best effort. People will notice if you do a good job. They will also notice if you give it only a half-hearted effort or drop the ball. By following through on your commitments, others will trust you. Trust is indispensable to success. It is the mark that others also have confidence in you. When others have confidence in you, they will alert you to new opportunities. People you don't even know might be observing what you're doing. Key players for your future may be hearing about you. Treat everything you do as if you are working in a small town where everyone will know what you did, and how well you did it.

Create opportunities for yourself if no one else is creating them for you. Ask for opportunities. By stepping out of the crowd, you have the chance to practice your skills in multiple arenas with players of varying skillsets. Some will be masters. Others will block you. Practicing by using opportunities allows you to learn how to navigate these twists and turns. Sometimes you will be effective and successful. Other times your learning will come from mistakes and outcomes that did not quite work out the way you envisioned. Either way, you will gain confidence as you learn from each opportunity. This confidence will set you up for your next success.

I have asked for every opportunity to create my path as I transitioned from humble beginnings to something more. I asked. I volunteered. I stepped up. I delivered and over-delivered—and continued to ask for more. Asking became my habit. I learned it was okay to ask. I learned how to handle rejection when someone said no. I found someone else and asked that person. This practice became valuable to building my confidence as I continued to progress in my skill development. It will be valuable for you too.

As I learned in gymnastics, each action builds on the other— then the other, and the other. By asking for more, my understanding of the working world and the people in it grew as I matured. I gained confidence. I understood I am capable. I am talented. I have a lot to offer.

You also have a lot to offer. You have enormous potential or you would not be reading this book.

Don't psych yourself out of discovering
your best opportunities. Don't limit
your possibilities for your future.
Be open to amazing possibilities.

Countless times over the years I have engaged in self-talk. Remember when I was recovering from surgery and repeated my mantra: *"I can, I will, I am, and I am going to?"* Self-talk has power. It makes your words more than an abstract goal. It makes it part of your mindset.

Focus your self-talk on things you will say and do. Want more. Believe you deserve more. Ask for more. Whatever your intention or goal is, say it out loud. Say it as if you mean it. Say it as if you believe it. Say it as if you know you will achieve it. This becomes your self-talk. Practice this in your car, your shower, and in your mind.

In the early days of owning my business, as a young self-employed management consultant, my biggest challenge was confidently asking for the sale. I was asking prospective clients to have the confidence in me to allow me the opportunity to solve their business problem. This was a big ask as those prospects had risks of their own to manage. Most were not willing to take the chance on me.

My fees for my management consulting work are generally based on project-oriented fees. However, it was not uncommon for people to ask me what my hourly rate was so they could pigeonhole the perceived value of my work. Essentially it was like asking you what kind of car you drive, and judging you by it.

Because by then I had honed my professional skills working for other management consulting firms, I was confident in my ability to engage in doing the client work. I also knew I was worth the fee rate I wanted to charge. In fact, I had so much moxie, I was asking for the same fee that my former firm had billed their client companies for my services. I figured if I was worth this rate to them, I was worth this rate to myself.

The problem was: I needed to be able say my price out loud with confidence since I was operating my own small business. When someone else was selling my consulting skills, they also were offering their own corporate cachet. I was now totally on my own. My clients were going to buy *me*. Separating a sales rejection from the rejection of my value as a person was hard.

To get ready for the inevitable question, I practiced my self-talk in my car while driving to the store, my business meetings or a networking event. Repeatedly as I drove, I would say, using various intonations, "My hourly rate is…, My hourly rate IS…, MY hourly rate is…," and I said the number.

The day my practice impacted my confidence arrived with an unexpected telephone call. I was at a board meeting in Connecticut, and in between meetings I went to my hotel room to check messages. I returned the call from one of Minnesota's most successful serial entrepreneurs. Ned had invested in multiple companies, which combined to reach $1 billion in revenue. Like most highly successful entrepreneurs, he could be challenging to deal with, and he was known to be a tough negotiator.

When my call went through, Ned and I talked at length about the consulting work he needed done. As we discussed my approach to solving his problem, I sold him on my ability to meet his needs. Ned then asked me the one question I had been waiting to hear, and practicing for, "What is your hourly rate?"

As I looked at myself in the hotel mirror, I knew I was ready. Without hesitating, I boldly stated, "My hourly rate is X." I shut up and held my breath.

Ned paused before responding, "Well, if that's your hourly rate, that's your hourly rate."

My eyes widened as I looked at my reflection. I asked for it and I got it. This successful serial entrepreneur was going to pay my market rate.

When we hung up, I was overjoyed and so proud of myself. I had been confident enough to close the sale and ask for the same hourly rate I had been worth to my former firm.

As I basked in the joy of my win, another thought occurred to me. Ned had responded so quickly to accepting my rate, I realized my price must have been lower than he would have been expecting to pay. I did not care. I was proud I had prepared for the moment. I did not verbally stumble through my answer when he asked the question. I had been ready. I was confident in my ability to respond. Like in my gymnastics lessons years earlier, my practice made me ready for the moment to handle it well under high-stakes pressure.

It also showed me my goal for setting my prices was too low. I re-assessed my consulting rates and raised them.

After I completed the work for Ned, his wife called me. We knew each other through mutually volunteering in a business organization, and she had originally introduced me to him. She was excited to tell me, "Ned was extremely pleased with the work you did for him."

I replied, "Yes, I know. He called and left that comment in a voicemail message."

She was dumbfounded, "He called you? Jill, he never calls anyone unless it is to complain. He *never* compliments anybody."

Ned's positive feedback added to my confidence in my abilities to succeed. I wish now I had saved his voicemail recording.

None of this would have happened if I had not compounded my confidence by practicing and preparing for the opportunity. I would have blown the sale with Ned if I had been wishy-washy about my fees rather than confidently stating them.

At the end of the day, it's you. It's you in the mirror, it's you on the phone, and it's you in the moment. You must be ready to say your words—after practicing them over and over.

I was ready. You will be too. This is the power of practicing.

Remember it takes time to learn new skills, so you need to factor time into how you will approach practicing your skills. Ask yourself:

- How much time do I need to invest?

- What people do I need to learn from?

- What resources do I need to save for or invest in?

- How long will it take for me to build on what I know or what I need to learn?

- What will it take to master my new skill?

- How will I practice?

Keep in mind you will have learning curves. There will be times when you're going to fumble and bumble. Your words won't come out perfectly. Or you will be so surprised when the opportunity presents itself that in the moment you won't be thinking clearly. Usually after the meeting is over, you will think of exactly the perfect thing to say.

Mistakes happens to everyone. You must always be willing to learn from the experience. No matter what the skill, you will need to practice.

I have missed opportunities in pitch meetings because the dynamic was off or there was a scary barracuda sitting at the end of the table that didn't want me brought in as a consultant. The barracuda would do everything possible to keep me off balance to make sure I did not present a strong-enough pitch to be chosen. In the early days, the barracudas were often successful in their endeavors. I would get rattled and lose the bid. By learning from these experiences, I became smarter and savvier every time I came up against one. Now I usually win.

So sometimes you'll blow it. It's okay. Chalk it up to a learning curve. Resolve to do better next time. Don't make a habit out of the failure. Don't let a mistake or lack of expertise shatter you. Move forward and learn from it.

Grieve Mistakes Briefly Then Go On

I operate under a 24-hour rule. I grieve about any business loss for a maximum of 24 hours. I evaluate what I could have controlled in order to win, and what I can improve next time. When my 24 hours is done, I begin looking for my next opportunity. I used to wallow in my failure for days. What a total waste of time and life spirit. Now I promise to do better, and let it go. So can you.

Remember if you lose out on an opportunity, there is always something else available to you. It might be an even better client or job. It might be someone who will appreciate what you have to offer even more. You can always find another opportunity. You must look for it. Shake the trees and find it.

You cannot take big leaps toward success unless you first take small leaps to build your confidence. The success you learn in those leaps compounds over time. By repeatedly testing yourself, and by preparing yourself for your next opportunity to win, you'll be ready because you're practicing your progressions. These two confidence keys are now intertwined.

In his classic book, *Outliers,* Malcolm Gladwell observed that it takes 10,000 hours of practice to become an expert or master a skill. Others dispute him about the amount of time it takes, proving even bestselling authors have critics. The number of hours doesn't matter. What matters is the knowledge and understanding that it takes time to build your skills to a deep level of mastery. Bottom line: it does not happen overnight.

Don't expect to be confident in the beginning. If you are, you are probably going to be over-confident and you will make huge mistakes. If you are in a job for 2,000 hours a year, taking two weeks of vacation each year, it could take you five years of full-time work to master a skill by using Gladwell's estimate. This is for one skill.

If you aspire to leadership in any area of your life, you need to invest time in each of the many components required to be effective. It takes less time to develop confidence. You may not master the skill, yet you can become more confident of your understanding of it without logging 10,000 hours of practice. You just need to break it down into smaller components so you can practice your progressions in more manageable chunks.

I hear all the time about people trying to fake what they know. You have heard the saying, "Fake it until you make it." This feeling you are faking often results in a phenomenon called the *"Imposter Syndrome"* where you have a deep fear that you will be exposed as a fraud. This fear will eat you alive and constantly undermine you. Experienced people will instinctively know you are lying or exaggerating. Don't try to mislead people about what you know, instead shift your focus on your continuing development and learning.

Make sure you don't undercut yourself either by *minimizing* what you know. This is the most significant reason why people feel like a fraud. They have so little confidence in themselves that they undermine their value. They feel unworthy or unable to accept credit for their skills or accomplishments. They fear success. Embracing your potential means more is expected of you. While it might be easier to limit your potential by sabotaging your winning, your disappointment will remain with you as a lack of confidence.

As you develop your confidence, you will need to consider what is next. Always have an ongoing focus as you practice. This will embed the skill deeply inside you so you can call on it with growing ease every time you need it. Then you can work on mastering it to developing the skill to a highly refined degree of finesse.

I am always looking ahead at what's next for me. Even now I still have more to do and more to achieve. I consider how I will prepare for my next level of success, consistently moving forward, developing new skills, and probing for deeper insights. I am searching to understand what it will take to propel me toward my next clients or my next leadership challenge. It never stops. Each one is a progression for me, as they will be for you.

My first management consulting job was with the Small Business Development Center (SBDC) at Drake University. I was pursuing my MBA because I had determined this master's degree was an essential educational credential to my becoming a management consultant. An announcement was made in one of my classes, saying the SBDC was looking for several MBA students to work with distressed businesses located throughout central Iowa during the terrible recession of the early 1980s.

I knocked a couple of people over as I ran out of the classroom to apply.

The program director hired me ten minutes into my interview. He could clearly see how much I wanted the job. More importantly, even at this young age, my business acumen was obvious. I had learned a lot from my family business, my part time jobs, and from my experiences in JA. I obviously understood how business principles applied to a small business. This gave him confidence to trust I already had more expertise than the typical MBA student, and could effectively impact their struggling clients.

I was not ready for big-time consulting as I still had a major learning curve. Working for the SBDC was my initial opportunity to start achieving my career goal. I spent many years working as a junior-level consultant in three different consulting firms to hone my professional skills. Ultimately, this preparation led me to have the confidence to establish my own management consulting practice.

Your skill development will occur in cycles. Sometimes the growth will be imperceptible to you. Often, we think we are at a plateau because we are not making larger moves. When this happens, keep in mind you are likely in a spiral of growth too subtle for you to see how far you have come. Spirals feel like you are just going in circles. When you are in a growth spiral, you are working in a gradually winding and continuous curve. You are deepening your abilities more than you realize. You are making movement and progress, but it is so hard to for you to see.

Sometimes you'll think, "I am not making progress at all." Yet you are. The truth is when you are working on a complex skill such as leadership, your progress often occurs in a flat spiral. This is because leadership has so many intricate elements intertwined in this skill. You need to simultaneously integrate each of the elements while you deepen your leadership mastery.

Frequently you are so close to the subtle spiral you will have a hard time realizing how far you have come. This is when feedback from a trusted friend, mentor or ally can provide you with the clarity you need. Reach out for feedback. Don't forget to return the favor to someone else. We all periodically wind up in the same slow boat.

Make the effort to find people who can provide you with new insights about other possibilities you may not have considered.

Don't rely only on your friends, peers, co-workers or family because they might not have any exposure to what you truly can become. Their narrow viewpoints could limit your potential.

Look for the people I call "Cardinals"—people who see opportunities beyond what is obvious to you. Those "Cardinals" can show you a future you might never have considered otherwise.

I met Robert Cardinal only once at a two-hour lunch in Chicago when I was preparing for the national JA competition. I know this was a throwaway meeting he did as a favor for a high school student who asked for the chance to learn from him to prepare for a business competition. Bob's words as he talked to me about his work became an inspiring "song" that ultimately transformed my ideas about future career options. He inspired me to pursue a bigger profession as he shared stories about his consulting career. No one in my small-town world could have provided this insight for me. I had to find this real-life Cardinal to learn what possibilities could be ahead in my future. Bob gave me the first insights I needed to find my wings so I could start to fly.

What I did not know until years after I met Bob was at the time we had lunch, he was the senior vice president of one of largest management consulting practices in the United States. It was an extraordinary confluence of events bringing him into my orbit. I took the opportunity to meet him. I also paid close attention to what he was saying. By listening carefully to what he shared, it changed my life.

When I was getting ready to celebrate the twentieth anniversary of my business, I started tracking down people who had impacted me throughout my professional career. I tracked down Bob, who had long since retired and is now living in Michigan. I wrote a letter to thank him. "Dear Mr. Cardinal, I know you have no idea who I am, but let me tell you how you have totally transformed my entire adult life." Briefly I shared with him what had happened in the intervening years.

I look for Cardinals everywhere. People who can inspire me, people who can test me, and people who can help me see what's my next possible opportunity. Find people who can do this for you.

As you see the greater possibilities for your life, you will begin searching to make them real. As you do this, you will build more confidence, and the sky can be your limit.

Chapter 5

Your Confidence Requires Daily Preparation

Confidence also requires boldness in action. If you're not taking action to build your confidence all the time, it will come and go in waves. When this happens, you will feel and act uncertain. You will not be sure of your abilities. Doubt will stall your progress and you will spin into irrelevant activities because they are easier than focusing on what you know you really should be doing. While working through your progressions, at each stage you must determine at a micro level what you need to do to be prepared for each movement. Your practice is your preparation.

Most people want to take shortcuts; however, the more thorough your preparation, the greater the likelihood is that you will have success. Preparation is especially essential to having confidence in yourself no matter what setting you are in—this will build your confidence when you are in high pressure situations such as interviewing for a job or dealing with higher-level bosses.

When I was in Junior Achievement in high school, we had many competitions. The one I mentioned earlier was at the national competition in Bloomington, Indiana. The contestants were from all over the United States and several foreign countries. I was the only girl of the six national finalists for President of the Year. I placed third and earned much-needed college scholarship money.

The phrase in my head at that time was the same one I had for gymnastics: *I can, I am, I will, and I'm going to.*

Today my mantra is, *"Why not me?"*

Who knows what my mantra will be in the next decade. I am sure I will still be chanting a mantra as I drive to another meeting.

All too often, we psych ourselves out of everything. "Oh, I can't be on this board." "I won't get this job." "Oh, I'll never be an executive." "I don't have what it takes."

Well, you know what? Everyone who achieves a high level of success at some point decided it was okay for him or her to achieve it. You have to ask yourself too, *"Why not me?"*

You can achieve success. You can earn a new job or attain an important goal, if you are prepared and ready for it when the opportunity presents itself to you—or if you go find one.

As you elevate, your opportunities will get tighter. Fewer people move on to reach the highest-level leadership roles. The ones who decide they will progress to higher rungs of success figure out a path to get there, and beyond. They're confident in what they know because they are prepared.

You can be confident too, if you prepare. Think big. Be bold. Take a risk. Prepare both your skills and your mindset to ensure success no matter how you define it.

Be very mindful of the people you invite into your life. Look for role models truly worthy of your respect. Let them shape your insights. Find people who authentically support you, who see more in you, and who challenge you to do better.

I met Lorelei Kraft when I was twenty-five. Lorelei was a fabulously successful serial entrepreneur. She was creating million-dollar businesses in an era when few women owned businesses. She was a pioneer. Even though she was extremely successful, Lorelei talked to me. I was a young nobody. She listened to me and answered my questions. She confirmed I was heading in the right direction. She could see potential in me I could not yet see. She boosted my confidence.

Allow yourself to connect. Successful people will talk to you and help you. Lorelei and I are still friends all these years later, as I am with many other people who have given me insights to build my confidence. Several of those people have died over the years, but they live on in my memories of their valuable advice. I continue to share their advice with others.

At times, you must face up to needing a tutor or some coaching to make progress in the right direction. I received a poor grade in my second-level required accounting class as an undergraduate business major. I had an expectation that someone else in my future workplace would do the debits and credits. My attitude was: I don't need to learn about these accounting details.

Silly me. I clearly had some maturing to do. I needed to apply myself to learning about boring concepts and studying topics outside what I thought I needed to learn. It was a hard lesson because my confidence was definitely not compounding, and it overheated and soon decomposed.

I did not make the connection at the beginning of my college career that information from the first-year courses were the building blocks for future classes. My initial failure was not learning enough in my first accounting class, which set the unstable foundation for the second. As a result, my initial error compounded by the time I was in the second-level class. I paid a high price for not working on my skill progression. My grade point average took a major hit, and my ego deflated. My parents were very unhappy. Digging out of this mess was all on me. It was hard, but I had confidence I could, and would, do better. I worked even harder to make my belief in myself come true.

By the time I was in graduate school working on completing my MBA, I had to take a managerial accounting course. I finally understood how relevant this class was to be successful in business. Since I was lacking the fundamental foundation for the topic, I studied harder and hired a tutor. I was so proud to earn an "A" on my first managerial accounting exam. It was a significant

Confidence Milestone.

After I completed my MBA and had begun my career in consulting, I became determined to work for one of the world's largest certified public accounting (CPA) firms. At the time, this environment was the best place for a career as a management consultant. I had figured out that working for a big CPA firm as a management consultant required a different skillset (and grades) than would be required for someone working in the tax or audit side of the business. I did not need to know about debits or credits to work on a market feasibility study. I wasn't asked about my undergraduate grades in accounting in my interview; only my MBA classes mattered. I knew I needed to be prepared to work hard to learn anything else I needed to know. I trusted my ability to learn. I was beginning to have professional confidence in myself.

Working in the CPA firm was a complex life experience. I was in a little over my head. I worked crazy hours trying to catch up and learn what I didn't know. It was hard enough to deal with what I needed to learn technically to do the work. Unfortunately, there were also challenges in working with the other members of my consulting team. They were all Type A personalities with big egos, and none of us knew how to work together effectively as a team.

It was a rough work environment. It was nothing like the platitudes I had read about in my business books sharing glowing stories of the wonders of the workplace and how everyone could make a difference. This real-life workplace was very different. I was struggling and highly stressed.

As I look back at it now, I was still in the early phase of developing a tough skin. I still needed to learn where the boundaries were for me and for others. At that point, I did not have the skill set to navigate this situation with ease.

Fortunately, I met Karen Marquardt, a CPA who worked in the auditing department of our firm. We quickly became friends, sharing insights about life and our careers. As I started to know her, I came to trust her. She also consistently provided me with wise counsel as I struggled to navigate the intricate challenges of my work team.

Some days were so hard. On those days, I would walk by Karen's cubical and whisper, "Fourth floor, now." I would continue walking out the door and take the elevator down to the bathroom located many floors below our office.

I had hit my wall. I knew I was going to cry. As a young woman in a male-dominated environment, I could not let anyone see me with a face full of tears. Karen would meet me in fourth-floor bathroom where she would help me re-group and plan what I would do to resolve whatever issue of the day had pushed me over the edge. I would splash some cold water on my face, pull myself back together, pump up my confidence, and go back to work.

I was enormously blessed to have had a work friend like Karen. She is still one of my closest friends and most trusted confidants. You need to have people in your life like Karen—people you trust enough to be vulnerable with, and who know you well enough to speak the cold hard truth to you in kind, but candid, ways to help move you forward. Trust me. Karen has said a lot of things to me over the years that were not fun to hear. However, I am a better business executive, management consultant, and human being because of her.

You need people in your life who see more in you than you see in yourself.

Peggy Lauritsen was the first client for my business. We were networking over lunch one day while I was still working at the CPA firm. Out of the blue, Peggy blurted, "I want to be your client."

I replied, "Great. I'll talk to my manager and we'll get a contract signed, and I will have them assign me to your account."

She responded emphatically, "No, no, no. I want to be *your client.*"

I responded in a reassuring voice, "Don't worry, Peggy. I know they will assign me to your account."

She grabbed my hands across the table and continued, "You're not listening to me. I want to be *your* first client, for *your* business."

I was flabbergasted—and I froze.

This was the ultimate moment of truth for me. I had been thinking about starting my own management consulting business for several years. I had been engaging in business development activities, which was why I was networking with Peggy. I had also been dreaming about it. It was as if my dream had been tattooed in neon ink across my forehead. For months people had been asking me when I was going to start my business. I laughed and always said, "Someday."

Until this moment with Peggy, I had not grasped that the right time had arrived. This day was now *my someday*.

Even though I had been saving for two years to have enough money so I could eventually start my own business, it was Peggy who gave me the final push I needed to leap so I could begin working with her to improve her business success. I had full clarity that I was ready to accept all the risks and work it would take to make my dream real.

Eight months later, I was fully out on my own as a management consultant when I founded Johnson Consulting Services. Peggy is still in business all these years later, and so am I. It all finally happened because Peggy saw more in me than I was ready to own and to accept. With her nudge, I was confident enough to take a chance on myself.

Chapter 6

Use Your Confidence Boosters

Finding ways to ensure that your confidence compounds also requires more subtle actions to allow you to maximize your opportunities to succeed. Think about the words you listen to, and determine if they are inspiring or damaging to your confidence. Consider whether you have the right coaches providing you with the feedback you need to build your skills. Find small mementos, tokens or talismans to ground you when you are unsure. Look for opportunities and consider the possibilities they offer you. Let's explore how each of these impacts your self-assurance and can give you a little confidence boost when you need it.

Words Influence Your Confidence

Make sure you are listening to words to build up your confidence. You should not need to listen to words undermining your self-assurance. We have enough negativity in our lives. Your self-talk might be sabotaging your confidence. Stop talking to yourself this way.

When the people around you say, "You're so talented in doing XYZ," please do not respond with the, "I Don't Deserve It–I'm Not Special" self-talk. Instead bask in the moment and allow the supportive words to become part of your spirit. Accept the feedback as a compliment and as acknowledgement of the results of your hard work. This is how you will build your confidence.

When you truly know, understand, and accept what makes you special, you will begin to believe it. Now you can move forward and act to leverage this skill to move you to the next level of success.

Buy or make a set of Confidence Cards with inspirational messages that are meaningful to you. Write yourself notes to remind you of your aspirations. These words will enable you to keep your focus on your goals or the skills you are trying to develop. Confidence Cards concentrate your mindset on the small golden nuggets you need to build your confidence day-to-day. They even can offer you gentle reminders to keep you grounded when your poise takes a hit.

Put your Confidence Cards in your wallet or on your bathroom mirror. Have the cards in your car so you can look at them for a quick confidence reminder before you go into a job interview or to a big client meeting.

I write myself reminder notes before I get on important phone calls. Those notes focus on key business points I want to make, and they also contain important messages with confidence reminders I might need.

Evaluate the voices you are listening to and the words they use. You may have people around you saying, "Oh, you'll never be able to do this. Why are you even trying?" Tune them out if they are your family. Walk away from them if they are your friends. Find another job if they are your employer. When you can, simply eliminate those people from your life. Surround yourself with people who expect more of you and demand you perform at a high-standard level. These people will help propel you to greater opportunities for success.

> ***You don't need to listen to people who tear you down. The most important voice you must listen to is your own.***

What you tell yourself matters. Make sure you tell yourself the truth about how you are doing. Be your own coach. Challenge yourself like you would if you were coaching someone in whom you saw great potential. Think about how you would encourage them. Now shift those words and encourage yourself. It will make a difference.

Have a "go-to" music playlist when you need a confidence enhancement. Combining inspirational words with uplifting music can often move your mind to a place where you can believe in possibilities. The music can help you imagine a new pathway to achieving your goals.

I love musicals because many of them are written about people who are seeking more or struggling through a hard time while still maintaining optimism for the future. This is why the song "Somewhere Over The Rainbow" from *The Wizard of Oz* resonates so strongly for people all these years after Judy Garland first sang it in the movie in 1939. My personal favorite is "The Impossible Dream" from *Man of La Mancha*. It has been my go-to song since I was in gymnastics. The lyrics about the quest to achieve the impossible dream always resonate with me.

When your mental voice pops up saying, "Oh my gosh, I suck. I'm not worthy. This is going to be a failure, this isn't going to work." Do a visualization to turn down the volume of the failure talk. Having a "you-suck" voice in your head is never going to help you succeed—nor is it going to build your confidence.

When you need to stop ruminating on negative thoughts, turn on some motivational music. Using your music playlist with encouraging messages helps program new thoughts into both your mind and your heart. These thoughts can be so powerful. Changing your thought patterns with music can move you beyond the harmful words in your head to put you back on a path toward success. Choose to hit the eject button on the negative self-talk in order to keep your confidence compounding.

Make a special music play list for those days when your confidence falters, listen to it and sing along with the words. What songs bring your mind back to the possible?

Find Coaches

Not everything I attempted in my life was a success. I decided I needed to take voice lessons when I was in my mid-twenties. I had done some amateur performing in college, as it was so much fun to sing and perform for others.

It was fun until the night I had a drunken heckler in the front row of my performance for a college talent show. Let's simply say it was not a great experience. I was the off-key singer who did not hit all the notes. My show set was a disaster. I was embarrassed while I was performing, which made me sing even worse. I was angry with myself for not being able to deal with the heckler better during the performance. I shattered in front of the audience. After the show, I stopped singing in front of people, and rarely sang except when I was alone in my car.

Of course, I had practiced singing my songs. Unfortunately, my practicing was done in a very safe and controlled setting. Yes, I thought about my presentation, how I would move on stage, and what I would wear. I had done my progressions before the night of the show by performing in front of other live audiences.

What I had not prepared for was how to handle my performance in a pressurized situation. I had not practiced for, or even considered, how I would handle a major distraction like this drunken idiot. I did not have the stage presence or presentation moxie to handle a challenging situation when I lost control of the room. I could sing, but I did not possess the technical expertise to control my breathing and vocal tone when I was under so much stress.

In the moment of my disastrous performance, I discovered how little I knew. It was a mortifying experience. I should have known better. My understanding about how to build my confidence had not already crystalized, and I did not have a strong coach guiding me. I was cocky and over-confident. I thought I was prepared, but I blew it big time in front of a lot of other people.

Several years later, I went through a phase where I was facing all my fears. I decided to address my singing disaster. I sought out the best vocal coach I could find in Minneapolis. I hired Oksana Bryn. She was a classically trained opera singer with an extraordinary voice and amazing presence. She had emigrated from the Ukraine to the United States after World War II. Oksana taught me so much about singing. She taught me even more about confidence.

Oksana discovered I have a four-octave singing voice, which apparently is quite unique. I learned from her that I could not have sung that night with poise when the heckler began his game with me because I did not have a solid foundation of experience. Nor did I have the technical skills developed to fall back on to ground me when the situation became rocky. Because I have such a wide vocal capability, I had selected challenging songs that tested my vocal control. Without solid technique, my unique vocal range became a weakness when my confidence was attacked. Oksana helped me understand I could never sing consistently until I had full confidence in myself, my technical skills, and my ability to control my emotions in front of an audience.

I began making the mental connections between managing how confident I was feeling and how I was projecting my voice. What Oksana taught me transcended our work each week on my singing skills. Her insights started overflowing into my meetings with clients, my work as a consultant, and my volunteer leadership roles. I accepted Oksana's correction notes and began practicing them daily. I started to trust myself. I brought this self-trust into how I approached dealing with my team members in the consulting firm. Oksana's insights compounded my growth far beyond what I had imagined I would learn by taking singing lessons.

During her time with me, I learned Oksana had been a very famous opera singer in Eastern Europe. Her career had been interrupted by the war. The life she knew, loved, and had prepared for as a performer ended without her consent. After she emigrated, Oksana lived a quieter life in Minnesota until she finally got her chance again. At the age of forty-five, Oksana performed a solo concert at Carnegie Hall in New York City. For a musician, performing at Carnegie Hall is the highlight of any career, and it was rare for someone her age to get the chance to perform there.

As she told me the story, I remarked, "Oksana, that must have been overwhelming. You must have been so scared."

She looked at me with an intense gaze and paused. She shook her head vigorously. Responding in her thick Ukrainian accent, she said, "No. I was not afraid because when I walked out onto the stage, I knew I belonged there."

Think about this for a minute. Oksana reflected total self-confidence as she spoke these words, *"I knew I belonged there."*

I wondered for years what it would feel like to finally feel this depth of confidence in myself. Many days, I wondered if this elusive feeling of self-assurance would even be possible. It took decades for me to integrate my skills and acumen with my confidence. As I was waiting at the bottom of the stairs to go up on the stage to accept the Women Industry Leader award from the *Minneapolis-St Paul Business Journal*, it finally hit me. I understood fully what Oksana had meant so long ago. I had accomplished what was needed to deserve this award. I had earned it through my determination, skills, and accomplishments. I knew with total clarity I belonged there. I walked confidently across the stage to accept my award as nearly 1,000 people in the audience applauded my achievement. This was another Confidence Milestone.

Look for coaches who will challenge you. As you think about where you are in your life, ask yourself: 1) what are your foundational skills and 2) where do you need more work? Now it's time to work on it. Go find the coaches you need to help you confidently build these skills.

Trust me, there will be a day when you finally have confidence enough in yourself for you to understand this, too. You belong here. It will be Oksana's gift to you, one she passed to me so I could to give it to you. Once you know what this means, you must share this insight with someone else coming behind you to help build their confidence.

Use Talismans

Another thing you can do to boost your confidence is to find deeply personal ways to ground yourself when your confidence wavers. For me, it is the image of a seagull. The seagull represents to me the achieving of an impossible dream or reaching another goal. My gymnastics club in high school was named Johnathan's Living Seagulls. The owner had named his gym after the famous book, *Jonathan Livingston Seagull,* written by Richard Bach. The book was about a seagull that was determined to learn to fly.

Seagull images were everywhere in the gym to remind us our dreams were possible. Our head coach, John, used the seagull image to help us learn to visualize our goals. At the end of practice, John would have us lie on the gym floor, have us close our eyes and imagine every aspect of accomplishing our future dream. Most of the little ones were dreaming about winning Olympic gold medals. I was dreaming about earning a coveted spot at the State gymnastics meet.

John demanded excellence in a sport based on a vision of perfection and the ability to manage the inherent dangers of gymnastics. John viewed dreaming big dreams as critical; however, he knew putting forward the day-to-day effort was essential to making any big dream a viable reality.

John taught me to how develop my self-confidence by doing my routines safely with style, grace, and technical perfection. He also drilled me to get back up quickly when I inevitably fell, and to keep going no matter what happened. He viewed failure as refusing to get back up and try again to do your best.

John's coaching discipline remains with me today. I follow John's approach in defining the excellence of my work. It permeates my approach to continuing to expand my expertise. It also is the foundation of how I continue to build my self-confidence in an increasingly complex business environment.

I still have big dreams for my future, and I continue to strive to do more and achieve more. The image of a seagull is on my business card, and it will always be my logo. My first client, Peggy, designed my logo decades ago. Whether it was in gymnastics or in business, to me the seagull is a visual representation of the possibility of achieving the impossible.

The seagull initially represented the impossible dream of starting my own management consulting business. Over the years, as I progressed through each new level of success, my impossible dream continues to be redefined to shift to something new. Every time I hand out a business card or a document with my seagull logo on it, I am passing along the essence of my impossible dream to another person. They don't know it, but I do. This is also why there is a seagull image on the front of this book. It is my subtle way to remind you that you can fly too and achieve your impossible dreams.

Yes, there will be times when your confidence falters. When this happens, you must find a way to self-comfort. An easy technique to do this is to wrap a blanket, a shawl, or a pashmina around yourself. The act of wrapping yourself is a powerful technique to provide self-nurturing and support. This is like the comfort you provide when you swaddle an infant. It provides you with a sense of security to help you regain your emotional balance.

Every day can be a struggle. A doubting voice can rise inside you saying, "I'm not sure if I belong in this room." It also happens to me. When I have my seagull talisman, it's a way for me to remind myself of who I am—and I do belong. This image quiets any negative self-talk and helps move me back to being confident. I have seagull images in my office. They hover over me while I work and serve as a symbol to remind me to believe in myself.

Find Your Significance

When your self-talk is, "Nothing I do is worth anything," you must find the value deep within yourself. If you don't value yourself, no one else will either.

No matter how small or how big your role is, think about how your job is transformative to those around you. What would be missing for them without the work you do? Consider your small value—and think about your bigger value. Ask yourself, "How does my work cascade and transform into touching other people? How do my efforts impact the greater vision of my company, organization or community?"

When I am working on solving a client's business issue, I know most of their employees will never have heard of me. Their customers will be using the services and amenities I said needed to be delivered. Client and employee lives will have been significantly touched by my recommendations. My management consulting work is impacting hundreds and thousands of lives exponentially, now and well into the future. However, personally I will be invisible to most of them. I don't need their validation to know my work matters. I leave my legacy with every client. I know my value.

You are like George Bailey in the classic movie, *It's a Wonderful Life*. Look for your value deep within, and when you find it is when your confidence will begin. This is also when your confidence can truly start to compound. Believe in the reasons you belong exactly where you are right now and in the future, with your job, your family, your community, and everyone else to whom you are connected. *You matter.*

Throw Rocks Across the Water

I have always loved skipping rocks across water. The movement of the ripples is mesmerizing because I never know where or how far they are going, or in which directions.

Building your confidence is also like this. Taking on new challenges and experimenting with different skills is identical to throwing the rocks across the water. Your experiences become the ripples. The cumulative impact of generating ripples becomes transformative. The ripples of where you throw your rocks will remind you of the progressions it takes to get to your desired result. You don't know exactly where the ripples will take you, but each ripple moves you closer to a more confident future and toward success.

Preparation and progression also remind me of baseball. Fans want to see the big home run all the time. But winning isn't always achieved by getting home runs. You can win consistently by getting one base hit, then another, then another and another. Base hits allow you to move from first base to second base to third base and then score a run. This type of win is achieved in smaller increments than a home run—and yet those base hits can still get you to the same winning result.

When celebrating my twentieth business anniversary, I spent a lot of time looking for people I had met early in my career prior to the advent of the Internet. I had no email addresses for many of them, and I had lost track of where their careers had gone. One person I wanted to reconnect with had been the former chief financial officer (CFO) for one of my clients which was one the nation's largest and most prestigious senior living communities. Rick lost his bid to become the chief executive officer (CEO) of the organization when the senior executive I worked most closely with for the client was selected for the CEO position.

Rick did what often happens in this situation, he left and went to another enterprise. I had never worked directly with Rick and had only limited interactions with him. Although I didn't know him, I decided it was the perfect time to reconnect, since he was now the CEO of a different organization. It had been four years since I had last talked to him. Rather than call Rick out of the blue, I put a hand-written note on my anniversary brochure and thanked him for being part of my first twenty years in business. I mailed the envelope and waited to see if I could create a ripple.

Two months later, Rick called, saying, "I have a small project I want you to come to Chicago to look at. We've been working on this deal for about six months, and we cannot figure out what to do about it. Will you come down for a day?"

Of course, I responded, "Yes."

Then he asked, "What's your daily rate?"

This was another career progression I was ready for as I was now even more confident in my professional skills. I was also more adept at answering the question about my fees and value.

I traveled to Chicago to meet with Rick and his leadership team. After reviewing their information about the potential project, I advised them to walk away from their deal because it didn't make business sense. The location was wrong, the market dynamics were wrong, and there was too much entrenched competition. Rick loved my candor. I had the confidence to speak truthfully. I also had developed the confidence to recommend killing a $200 million deal in a single day.

Because of the success of this one day with Rick and his team, I was hired for another small project with his organization. This led to working for them on a huge consulting engagement in Seattle. I was competing for the Seattle project against several nationally known consulting firms. Winning this bid was a huge breakthrough for my company. This win created another Confidence Milestone. My successful work in Seattle resulted in them hiring me for another consulting engagement for their corporate office.

Had I listened to my "Don't do it" voice, I would have missed out on a very nice chunk of business as well as a powerful business relationship. I went forward with confidence, and it compounded right into my bank account.

What I did not know until we started working together in his new position was that Rick had read every single report I had prepared while he worked as the CFO for my previous client. He already knew the quality of my work and the level of detail I review for my clients, but I never knew he was so familiar with my consulting expertise.

If I had listened to my self-talk to not send the note to Rick, I would never have renewed this relationship. By doing a "What the heck" and reaching out to him, I scored a win. I found this small bold action paid immediate dividends. Those dividends continue to benefit me even to this day. My bold action with my little handwritten note was golden, and was worth a lot of money to my business.

Rick also threw rocks across the water as he regrouped from losing out on the job he wanted. He found another path to becoming a CEO.

All successful people find another way when their path is blocked. You can too. Keep trying.

Chapter 7

Be Wary of Golden Handcuffs

In the business world, "golden handcuffs" are the lucrative benefits employers offer as an incentive to discourage employees from taking another job. You can also think of golden handcuffs as *those thoughts holding you back from pursuing your goals*. Golden handcuffs in this sense can be the security of a paycheck or the safety of remaining in your hometown. These golden handcuffs are the psychological shackles of your life preventing you from daring to take the necessary risks to achieve your goals.

> *When you have the chance to make your dream come true, grab it with both hands. Don't let the golden handcuffs keep you where you are—or to hold you back from fully embracing your success.*

Don't let your fears psych you out before you see what you are truly capable of achieving. Sometimes it may not be the right time for you to achieve your goal…yet. Occasionally you will need a little help to prepare for it. Don't let your ego get in the way of asking for the support you need. Often the real reason you are unwilling to accept the opportunities presented to you is because *you are the roadblock to your own success.*

Grab Opportunities

One of my friends had the perfect career opportunity come his way. He'd prepared for it, and he was experienced enough to take on this new responsibility. The biggest stumbling block initially appeared to be the job requirement to move to California from the upper Midwest.

James and I met to talk about his options over dinner. After he talked about the inconvenience of the potential move, he finally revealed his real reservations about taking the job. He expressed the typical negative self-talk of someone who still lacked confidence. He invented reasons to hold himself back from accepting the job. He repeated, "I can't take this position, because I am not ready."

As I listened to him talking himself out of accepting the opportunity, I finally understood the right words to say to him. I leaned in and quietly said, "James, it's okay to unlock your golden handcuffs. None of these reasons matter enough *not to take this job.*"

I encouraged James to give himself permission to decide he could go. He had always wanted to work in California. This was his dream job and the dream opportunity to implement many of his innovative professional ideas. I advised him to "Grab this opportunity with both hands…and go for it."

James faced his fears, accepted the job, and moved to California. This turned into the best professional decision he has ever made. He has earned a glowing national reputation in his field. He is traveling all over the world. James is finally living his dream because he had the confidence to accept a golden opportunity when it was presented.

We all lock ourselves up with golden handcuffs. When you hold yourself back, you will never know what you were truly capable of accomplishing. You do not have to set limits for yourself. You do not have to tell yourself to stop trying. You can propel forward to act to achieve your big dreams. Even if you don't fully reach them, it doesn't matter. *What matters is that you will go farther than if you did nothing.*

Don't let your ego handcuff your opportunity for success. You have the potential to be transformative to your enterprise, to your community, and to your family. It is simply a matter of re-framing your mindset to tell yourself, *"I can, I will, I am, and I'm going to."* Then do it.

Timing Is Everything

Not everything you try will work. This does not mean you should stop your efforts. Sometimes the real issue is: this is just not your time…right now.

The first time I tried to get appointed to the board of directors for our state's Chamber of Commerce, I received a polite "thanks but no thanks" rejection letter. I was upset because I had prepared and I was confident. I was mentally ready for the leadership responsibility. I had worked hard as a volunteer and contributed significantly to the organization. I had successfully chaired one of the organization's major committees. I was routinely presenting to the board and working with them. I felt I had earned the right to attain this prestigious board role. I could not believe I had been passed over.

One of the people I vented to about this rejection was a Chamber board member I had gotten to know from all the board meetings I attended. Valerie Pace was an executive in a Fortune 100 company, and she had served on this board of directors for a long time. She listened patiently to me complain about the rejection letter.

Valerie nodded to affirm the unfairness of the situation before she gave me some extremely valuable insight. She explained, "Jill, it's almost impossible for a small business owner from the metropolitan area to get on this board. The organization has to save those spots for the big companies because they pay the bulk of the membership dues."

She paused and said firmly, "Submit your name for consideration again next year."

I thought Valerie was nuts. If they had not taken me for the board now with all the things I had accomplished for the organization, what difference would a year make? Why would they take me next year if they did not think I was good enough now?

I was such a dope. I nearly let my ego get in the way of my potential for success. Valerie was right. It was never an issue of my not being the right fit for the board. Nor was it about me not being good enough. It was merely an issue of the timing and the limited board slots they could fill with someone like me.

I was named to the Minnesota Chamber of Commerce Board of Directors the following year. Valerie taught me a powerful lesson: you must keep trying.

> *Do not give up on something you want to achieve and feel you have earned. Sometimes you do have to be patient and wait your turn for the proper timing.*

Make sure you stay in the game.

Invest in Getting Help

Having highly developed self-awareness is key to knowing how far your confidence will take you in work and life. Sometimes your own confidence won't be enough. Asking for support may not be enough. You may need to hire the proper expertise to achieve a goal.

A passion of mine over the years has been raising and showing Rottweiler dogs. One of my first Rottweilers was a stunning dog that was beautiful both inside and out. Everyone could see my Kadi was a show dog, and we all knew she would be a champion. Kadi had confidence, along with a winning presence and exceptional conformation.

To give your show dog the greatest chance of winning, the person showing it must be able to bring out the dog's best in the show ring. If you've ever watched the American Kennel Club competitions on television, you know the show ring is nerve wracking. Competing to win requires compounded confidence on the part of both the handler and the dog.

Despite practicing and taking classes, I was a terrible handler in the show ring. I could compete in the obedience ring. Unfortunately, no matter what I did, I could not get the hang of making Kadi look good in the show ring. I was holding her back. I finally had to admit show ring handling was not a skill I could develop with the confidence required to allow Kadi to succeed.

Admitting my lack of skill in this area was difficult, and hiring someone to do it for me was going to be expensive. I needed professional expertise to earn Kadi's title since getting more training was not working for me. I invested in hiring a professional handler.

Brian started working with Kadi as her handler on a Saturday, and they competed together over the next several days—and began winning. By the following Thursday, Kadi had completed her championship title. Brian had her for only six calendar days. I had been chasing her championship title for nearly three years. It took someone who knew what he was doing, and who had the juice with the judges to get her looked at seriously in the ring, to achieve a highly sought-out goal in the dog world in only six days.

Winning her first championship title led to an amazing show career for Kadi and she became one of the nation's top Rottweilers. I successfully competed with her in the obedience ring, and we earned several obedience titles in the U.S. and in Canada. Kadi ended up earning a spot in the Rottweiler Hall of Fame. It was a powerful lesson in letting go and investing in help to achieve a goal.

Chapter 8

Present Yourself Confidently

Confidence fuels your desires and big goals. Unfortunately, you need more than fuel to achieve success. Beyond preparing, you need to allow others to recognize your potential. This means you need to become comfortable with allowing people to see you in action.

Successful people are not invisible. Confident people do not hide in the shadows. It is hard to get comfortable with learning how to present yourself confidently to others. Presenting yourself confidently requires self-trust. It also requires, you guessed it: practice. Here are several actions you can take to present yourself with more confidence.

Step Into the Spotlight

Allow people to see what you can do. Allow them to begin imagining what else you might be capable of doing. If your talents and potential are not visible, no one will emerge to open doors to opportunities for you.

79

When I was in high school, I practiced stepping into the spotlight. I was involved in dancing and was a gymnast. I was in forensics (speaking competitions) where I learned to speak in front of small groups. I was even a majorette twirling fire batons at half-time during our high school football games. I would practice lighting my baton on fire and twirling it in my dad's body shop because it had a high ceiling. I would try to hit the ceiling, and then catch the baton before it landed on the floor, without burning my hand. It was a mental game to make the drudgery of my practice more fun.

All of this was about learning to perform in front of other people. I sought out audiences to build my confidence. Heck, I was willing to twirl my fire baton in front of the customers in the body shop if they would watch me do it.

You must let people see you if you want to advance. It takes tons of practice to become comfortable standing in front of other people. It takes practice in many different arenas to build your confidence so you can trust yourself enough to stand alone in the spotlight.

Own Your Abilities

You need to identify, enhance, and believe in your own abilities. If you don't, why should anyone else? Don't assume people will recognize and reward your talents. You need to own them first yourself.

Owning your abilities will build your confidence for when you get into a pressure situation.

I recall entering a prestigious private club for a meeting right after had I started my business. I saw some very strange looks from people who were coming out of the building. Those stares were a bit unnerving. In a moment of insecurity, my immediate thought was they did not think I belonged in this fancy private club.

The gaze of one of those people looking at me went down to my feet. As I followed this stranger's downward glance, I caught a glimpse of color as I was walking. With a start, I realized I was wearing two different colored shoes, a red one and a black one. The electricity had gone out in my apartment that morning. Because I was running late and in a hurry to get to my client appointment, I just stuck my feet into the dark closet to put on my shoes before running out the door. They were the exact same shoe style, but just in different colors.

It was nearly time for our meeting to start, so it was too late for me to run home to change my shoes. This was a moment of truth for me, and I had to deal with this. I rearranged my attitude and let go of the feeling I did not belong. I confidently walked in the front door of the private club and went into my meeting room displaying strong and confident body language. I reframed the situation in my mind so I would project confidence as I went into my client meeting. I decided those mismatched shoes were my red ruby slippers like Dorothy wore in the *Wizard of Oz*. I owned it and laughed about it with my client. I did not let the small mistake of mismatched shoes destroy my self-worth, or my confidence in my abilities.

I can, I will, I am, and I'm going to….

Project an Executive Presence

Your posture and facial expressions play an important role in helping you become more confident. You need to look, act, and speak with confidence. People who project confident body language are listened to more carefully. Standing tall or sitting up straight when you speak conveys an air of confidence.

Look at how you handle yourself when you are dining with others. You may discover you need to work on your table manners and etiquette. Most of us have learned this as we moved through our career, and few of us learned these techniques at home. Like me, you may need to learn how to do this with confidence. I read a book, and I watched how others used their silverware. I figured it out. It will be easier and faster for you to learn this because of all the video clips available on the Internet.

Years ago, I had a mentoring lunch with a young man with huge aspirations for his future. Chris and I had a long conversation about his professional options and how to tackle his networking efforts. All throughout the luncheon, I was distracted by his table manners. He was using the wrong silverware and jamming his fork into his food like he was trying to kill it. I knew this was how Chris ate at home, and these were completely involuntary actions on his part. I gave him the candid feedback he needed at the end of the meal and recommended a set of online videos to watch. He watched them and began working diligently on getting comfortable using the techniques demonstrated by the etiquette expert. Chris is now a seasoned executive with an enviable network of clients and colleagues. Today his executive presence reflects the total package of professional savvy and confidence.

Communicate Effectively

I know this is a shock, because we all expect the people in our lives to always know what we are thinking. However, they often don't understand us because we are unclear. Don't expect people to be clairvoyant and read your mind about what you want. Don't expect them to figure out what you are trying to say. If you don't communicate effectively, those listening to you cannot read your mind. Whether your audience is a full room or someone you are talking with one-on-one, be clear.

Spinning in uncertainty is senseless when a question or two can get you to clarity. If you don't know something, ask. If you are confused about an instruction or request, ask. If you are unsure about competing priorities, ask. *Asking is part of effective communication.* Just make sure you also listen carefully to the answer.

Be prepared and ready to get to the point quickly when you are speaking. Think through what your point is rather than talking all around an issue until you finally determine what you want to say. If you don't speak with fully formed ideas or self-assurance, trust me, people will stop listening to you or cut you off. This is especially important if you're dealing with higher-level executives or people in power positions. They are under too much stress, and have too many demands on them. Don't waste their time. You will lose confidence when you realize no one is listening to you.

Speak up. Be clear. Own the room by communicating clearly with confidence. Sometimes you must continue to communicate with confidence even when you feel awkward or uncomfortable. How you own your confidence in a moment when your poise is lacking will be your ruby-slipper moment. It is not always easy to communicate when your confidence fades.

I ran the Book Club at the Minneapolis Club for over sixteen years. The Minneapolis Club is one of the nation's preeminent private clubs. Its members are high-level executives and powerful community leaders. I was honored to be a member. My primary volunteer role there was moderating the Book Club meetings where members talked about whatever non-fiction book I had selected for the month's discussion. Club members were welcome to attend any meeting they wanted. Some members came regularly, while other came to only one luncheon. It always varied, and I never knew who would show up for the discussion.

I had been intrigued by a book I had found about Ernest Shackleton and his disastrous 1914 expedition to Antarctica. I thought it would be of interest to our Club members, so I put it into our reading rotation. I prepared for the meeting with my normal diligence, and made many notes so I had good questions for the group to discuss.

I arrived early and waited for the day's participants to arrive. Several older professional men came in the room. Since I didn't know who they were, I walked around the room to introduce myself.

As I was shaking one man's hand, he said his name. I did not know who he was, so I asked, "And where do you work?"

He responded simply, "I work at 3M."

This was impressive as 3M is one of the world's largest companies. I was excited, "My mom used to work at 3M. What do you do?"

He smiled and said, "I'm the CEO."

Life stopped. This was another ruby-slipper moment. I took a second to regain my composure. As I did this, I clarified my thinking. Not knowing such an important business leader by sight was not going to unravel me. Book Club was my room, and I was completely prepared for our book discussion. I was there to run a meeting to discuss a terrific book about an amazing event in history. Without missing a beat, I responded, "Wow, your mom must be really proud of you."

Seriously, what else could I say? He laughed, and so did the man who was standing next to him.

I turned to him and asked, "How about you?"

He replied, "I'm retired now, but I used to work at 3M."

By now, I was in on their joke, "And what did you do for 3M?"

He smiled and answered, "I used to be the CEO."

It was a heck of an icebreaker. It had likely been quite a long time since someone had come into their orbit who did not instantly know them by face or name, but was confident enough to not worry about it.

At my Book Club luncheon that day, I had three Fortune 100 CEOs and the billionaire CEO of one of the world's largest privately-held companies in the room. Honestly, if I hadn't been so well-prepared, my luncheon would have been a disaster. I masterfully orchestrated the discussion of the book. They all were totally engaged in the conversation that I was clearly in control of; it was *my room*. They all knew it, accepted it, and looked to me to expertly guide their discussion.

Afterward, the billionaire CEO went to the Club's general manager and said, "This is a world-class book club."

This became was my Atta Girl moment, and I happy danced in my red-ruby slippers.

Because I can, I will, I am, and I'm going to ... You can too.

The Essence of Confidence

Confidence is the balance point between being meek and brash. Taking a meek approach makes you timid and submissive. Taking a brash approach makes you aggressive and overwhelming to others. Confidence falls in the middle. To find your poise, you navigate between these two extremes. Here's where you can project a confident and self-controlled presence. Not too submissive and not too over-confident. This is the essence of confidence.

I have always loved this quote. I found it years ago on the outside of a sugar packet while I was having lunch with my dad in a rural diner:

> *"He who has a thing to sell and goes and whispers*
> *in a well is not so apt to get the dollars as he who*
> *climbs a tree and hollers."* – Author Unknown

It does not matter what you are selling. You could be selling widgets or consulting services. You will always be selling yourself and your ideas. You don't have to holler. You must ask for the sale, the promotion, the raise, and ask for the opportunity. If you don't speak up, you'll never get what you're looking for.

Every time I need a little confidence boost, I smile and remember tucking the sugar packet into my pocket. Bobby Johnson's little girl found the right words to continue reminding me to keep moving forward toward my next future success.

Put this message on one of your Confidence Cards. You, too, can use this little sugar packet reminder for yourself.

Learn to Control Your Emotions

Everything you're doing is building your personal brand. It is in how you deliver what you do. It is in the consistency of how you deliver it. It is in the package of how you present yourself. One other critical aspect of your personal brand is how you deal with your emotions. As you learn to manage your emotions, you will gain emotional maturity, and this will enhance your confidence.

You need to control your emotions rather than let your emotions control you.

During my early days in business, I hadn't developed consistent emotional control. It's why Karen would take me the fourth-floor bathroom for my meltdowns. I didn't want to break down in front of the people who matter—or when someone said, "You may not be qualified."

Trust me, those words and situations triggered a lot of emotion in me. I learned how to handle "moments" like this so they would not derail me. I stopped letting them overtake my emotional control. I learned how to recognize when my emotions were triggered and how to manage them before they lurched out of control.

Many times, our emotions set limits for what we can be, what we can do, and how high we can fly. We can set the ceiling for ourselves if we are emotionally out of control, rather than having limits set by the people around us. We can take rejections so personally it spins into a repudiation of our entire life and value. Stop it.

Learn to control your emotions. Move through these emotional episodes by utilizing some of the self-nurturing suggestions discussed earlier. As you neutralize your emotional instability, then you can refocus your efforts on compounding your confidence. Once you begin to master your emotions you can address the self-limiting beliefs preventing you from moving even further down your success path.

Do not let anything stop you, whether it is a glass ceiling or an imaginary one. No matter your gender, race or where you come from early in life, break the damn glass.

> ***Shattering glass ceilings is about not letting other people define you. It is about you defining your future for yourself. Do not be your own glass ceiling.***

Fear and Self-Doubt

Confidence is the gap between our dreams—and believing we can achieve them. We all get stuck at various times in our lives. We all have self-doubts. Self-doubt is poison to confidence. Self-doubt is often triggered by fear. Fear is a powerful emotion. It is an emotion that can cause you to hold yourself back or sabotage your success. Fear can amplify your feelings of inadequacy. Fear can paralyze you from taking the actions you know are necessary to move forward.

Your confidence will fluctuate because of fear and self-doubt. In some environments, you will feel like you can conquer anything, and in other places you will feel like you should have just stayed in bed. When this happens, something is going on deep within you. This is the time to step back and reflect or to reach out to a trusted confidant. Allow yourself to embrace the stillness of a momentary plateau.

Many of the executives and entrepreneurs I consult with have moments of sheer terror. When they reach out to retain me, it is usually because something is not working right. These leaders need to project appropriate confidence to others to prevent their fears from spreading throughout their organization. No matter the face they put out to the world, they are still deeply concerned that the consequences of their decisions or the changing market forces they cannot control will cause them to fail. At their level, the stakes are high.

The truth is, the stakes are high no matter what level you are at when you are afraid. Confidence isn't going to magically appear because you want it. It's going to be within you because you work for it and you look for it. You face your fears and doubts. Then you move forward to try again.

A few years ago, I was having a lunch meeting with a renowned woman executive who was fifteen years ahead of me in her career. Over our meal, I revealed my deep secret, "I've blown it. My career is over."

I was struggling with my business and nothing I did seemed to be working. My sales had stalled. I felt like a complete failure. I was afraid I had finally hit the end of my success path.

Cindy looked at me very quizzically for a minute and then she started to laugh a gut-busting laugh. She was laughing at me...not with me.

Of course, this was not at all the reaction I was looking for from her. I had revealed my big fear, and I was feeling very vulnerable. I was expecting at least a little show of support.

When she stopped laughing, Cindy leaned forward and said, "Oh, for God's sake, get over it. Jill, you're fine. Do something. Push through this."

This was exactly what I needed to hear. Cindy's push moved me from being stuck to moving myself forward to take some new actions to get my business momentum moving again.

I realized later that all my practicing and progressions were working. I was stuck because I was moving through a transition to my next level of success. It was a big transition and I was still afraid I was not ready for it. I needed to keep doing what I was doing. I needed to push through the last bit of resistance to claim my spot. I needed to be confident in myself to know and believe what I was doing was the right thing to do. I also needed to stop relying on getting my validation from others. This was the real breakthrough moment for my confidence.

Confidence can fluctuate from day to day. Sometimes you are on the top of the world. The next minute you are trying to pick yourself up because you fell to the floor.

We all have self-doubt. We all have moments of fear and anxiety. Use those moments to be self-reflective. Wrap yourself in your blanket or pashmina. Figure out what is going on in your mind that is terrifying you and undermining your confidence.

Once you understand why you are stalled, push through your fear to move forward and act. Give yourself a time deadline. Whenever I am stuck or afraid, I determine what my next bold move needs to be. I take a deep breath and act on it before noon that day. Sometimes I get brave and will do second bold move. This can make me confident enough to do a third bold move or more.

If you can set a small bold goal and execute it before noon, you're done with it for the day. If you do one a day, you will do at least five actions before the end of your workweek. This weekly total will compound to over 250 by the end of the year. It will be 365 if you include weekends too. At least one of your bold actions will move you forward. More likely than not, the compounded effort of these daily bold actions will propel you farther and faster than you can imagine today. Break it down into one smaller bold action you do each day. This daily effort will soon become a habit to help build your success.

> ### *What do you have to lose by trying? You need to move through your doubt and fear so your confidence can compound.*

Keep working at it and chanting to yourself, *"I can, I will. I am, and I'm going to."* Then do it.

Chapter 9

Develop Your Own Confidence Plan

Now you are ready to begin developing your own Confidence Plan. Spend some time thinking through the following questions. You can also get a copy of the *Compounding Your Confidence Workbook* I have developed for my clients to aid them in compounding their confidence. You can find it on my website (www.jcs-usa.com). Either way you approach this, the key is to begin reflecting on where you are now, where you want to go, and how you are going to get there. Here is the framework of some questions you can use to develop your Confidence Plan.

Review your personal timeline:

- What is your history from the start of your career to now? Consider your family of origin, your jobs, your advisors, etc.

- What have been the key elements allowing you to get from there to where you are now?

- What strengths or skills have you begun to develop?

- What has blocked your success?

• What has undermined your confidence?

SWOT: Do a personal assessment. Ask others who know you well for their feedback. Be honest and detailed to assess your SWOT. Review your:

• Strengths

• Weaknesses

• Opportunities

• Threats

Vision:

• What can you see as the vision for your future?

• Who do you want to be in five years? In 10 years? In 20 years?

• Where are you at now in your life relative to achieving your vision?

Skills Assessment:

• Do your skills match your vision?

• What skills are you already working on that you will need to progress to your next level of success?

• What skills do you need to develop to get to the success level beyond the one you are trying to achieve now?

• What skill gaps do you need to fill in to progress?

- How will you gain those skills?

Patterns:

- What current patterns in your life are helping you to sustain a certain level of functioning?

- What are the patterns impeding your progress?

- What are the new patterns of behavior you need to develop to take the next leap?

- What do you need to let go of in order to move forward?

- What relationships in your life need to change?

- How can you better manage your fear and self-doubt?

Investment:

- What are you willing to invest to achieve your goals?

- What are you willing to invest to learn new skills?

- How much do you need to invest in terms of money?

- What do you need to invest in terms of effort?

- What other resources do you need?

- How will you get these resources?

Time Paths:

- What is your time path for moving forward?

- How can you better invest your time to achieve your vision?

- How can you break down how you spend your time into smaller increments to better achieve your goals?

Action:

- What are three actions you can do now to help you move forward?

- What are three actions you can do now to help you break through to the next level of success?

- What can you leverage to create more opportunities?

- What else do you need to improve?

Grab a notebook and start jotting down your thoughts. Keep going back to your notes over and over. By deeply reflecting on these questions, you will learn more about yourself. You will see the patterns in thought and behaviors that undermine your confidence. Keep a written record of your plans so you can monitor your progress. Take corrective action when you need to find a better method to bolster your skilled development.

Create your Confidence Plan and implement it by taking action. Build your confidence and your future on a solid foundation of preparation. Build it on a foundation of knowing yourself. Continue to work on your progressions. Keep moving through those stepping-stones.

When you have laid a solid foundation
of preparation, step into the light
and let others see how you shine.

At times in my management consulting practice, I bid on engagements I want to work on—but don't get. Not everything works. No matter what the outcome, each time I am in a sales situation, I am learning golden nuggets I can bring to the next complex sale I am involved in, and what I learn increases my chances of winning the next big proposal.

As I navigated my business development when I was transitioning to work with more sophisticated clients, I often came in second place in the final round for high-fee engagements. I was very frustrated because it happened repeatedly. Second place does not pay my bills. Rather than wallowing in my failure, I asked my prospective clients what had caused me to be in the second-place—and what would have made me have a winning proposal. Most of them took the time to answer my questions. My prospective clients on those failed sales gave me exceptionally valuable insight I still use today when I am preparing a proposal for a consulting or speaking engagement.

Every part of my success is based off a solid foundation. Even though I have mastered many skills, I am always learning new ones or further expanding my expertise. Knowing I can learn builds my confidence. This ensures I can continue to be successful as I pursue new and different opportunities. It will be the same for you.

Develop a commitment to enhancing your skills. The more you enhance your skills, the more your confidence will grow. This is vital to executing an effective Confidence Plan.

You must want to accomplish your goals. You must have the hunger to drive you to the actions needed to achieve them. If you do not have a drive deep within you of wanting something more or something bigger, I can tell you with certainty, it will not magically find its way to you.

You can only sustain the actions necessary to achieve success if you have the personal commitment to following through on the progressions, practice, and presentation skills necessary to attain, and sustain, success.

You must want something bigger than what you have now. You need to allow yourself to want something more. First you need a vision of it or at least a glimmer of what it might be before you can find ways to create your own path and take the next step, and the next one.

Your step doesn't have to be the big step someone else might aspire to—but it must be a big step for you. You must own the boldness of your desire for more and make it part of your compounding confidence.

Chapter 10

Final Thoughts

Confidence is something you will work on your entire life. Keep trying new things. Stay resilient, even when you think you cannot be in a zone of self-assurance. Be mindful of how you progress. Work on your skills whenever you can to build your confidence. Keep practicing so you improve how you present yourself to others. Learn to present yourself confidently in front of others.

The compounded impact of taking small bold actions does not take a lot of time. But these small actions can morph into amazing opportunities with the potential to transform your future. Don't waste any more time.

When I was 16, I was selected as the North Hudson Pepper Fest Queen. I learned many lessons as I traveled to parades on behalf of my community.

The most important lesson I learned from being a queen was if you don't hold your head up, your crown falls off.

Confidence is also like this. Hold your head up whenever you are feeling self-doubt. Be willing to try new things and not succeed, but to learn from it. Be proud you made the effort to improve yourself. Then try again.

My parents had many plans for what they were going to do when they retired. Unfortunately, they both died at the age of sixty-four within just eight months of each other. They were never able to act on what they dreamed about for their retirement. They put off so much—and suddenly it was too late.

You don't know what can transform your life in an instant. Don't wait. Life is too short. You owe it to the world to leave your legacy. Your talents and gifts matter. When you are emotionally broken down, get up. You can be resilient and try again.

During your next transition, unshackle your golden handcuffs. Find your own golden egg. Look for your own pony. Find the skipping pebble to create the ripple moving through your life to provide yourself with transformative opportunities.

Opportunities are all around you, if you make it a priority to look for them.

I believe in you. Why? Because I believe anyone can compound his or her confidence. We all have the same number of hours in a day. The key is to focus your efforts on the little details of the actions you take each day. Your focused effort, compounded over time, creates new habits to prepare you for increasing levels of success. When you develop habits focused on doing better each time, this shifts your mindset. Your mindset eventually becomes the foundation for how you conduct yourself in life and how much you can achieve.

Take control of your destiny. Take advantage of those unexpected moments when opportunities appear for you. Act boldly to create new opportunities for yourself. No matter what, keep moving forward so your confidence keeps compounding. Then reach your hand back to help someone behind you build their confidence to join you on this success journey.

I don't know your future, but I do know this: if you own it, act on it, and you make it yours, you will compound your confidence. By implementing your Confidence Plan, you will find the path to take you on the journey to your golden future.

You can, you will, you are special,
and you are going to succeed.
The next steps are yours. Take them.

P.S. Let me know how you have made your Confidence Compound. You can join the **Compounding Your Confidence Facebook Group** to connect with me and others interested in building their confidence. I look forward to hearing from you.

About Jill

An award-winning management consultant, Jill J. Johnson has personally impacted more than $4 billion worth of business decisions through her consulting work. She is in the board rooms, the back rooms and the executive suites where complex decisions are being made, impacting the future of clients located throughout the United States, as well as in Europe and Asia. She knows what it takes to develop and implement strategies for turnarounds or growth that get results.

Jill is a widely-respected business executive and leader who has been a member of the boards of directors and executive committees of a variety of business, professional, and governmental boards. She has served on two federal boards under three different United States presidents representing both political parties.

Jill has won numerous honors for her business acumen, her leadership savvy, mentorship skills, and her entrepreneurial successes. Jill is also one of the first women ever inducted into both the Minnesota Women Business Owners Hall of Fame and the Top Women in Finance Hall of Fame.

Over the years, Jill has been quoted on a range of management issues in national publications including *The Wall Street Journal, The New York Times, Inc., Money Magazine* and *Entrepreneur.* She has appeared as a thought leader on a variety of radio and television programs for business. She is a 4th generation entrepreneur who grew up in a family-owned business.

Jill is a powerful speaker with the rare ability to deliver substantive content in a way that is engaging and easily accessible. She is also a Professional Member of the National Speakers Association.

Jill resides in Minneapolis, Minnesota.

Talk to Jill about how her Consulting Services can help you gain the clarity you need to develop your business strategies. Book Jill to Speak at your next event. Contact her at:

www.jcs-usa.com

www.twitter.com/JillJohnsonUSA
www.facebook.com/JohnsonConsultingServices
www.linkedin.com/in/JohnsonConsultingServices

Acknowledgments

Thank you to everyone who encouraged me to share my stories about how to build your confidence with the world. You made this book possible.

To my audiences:

To the audiences who responded so strongly to the messages contained in this book. Thank you for telling me how much this insight has meant to you and for encouraging me to share it with others.

To my book team:

Jan McDaniel for helping me pull together my ideas as I pieced together this book. You helped me put my words to paper.

Connie Anderson for your spot-on editing advice. I am glad I allowed you to coach me!

Chris Mendoza for the cover design and formatting to turn my idea into a reality.

Ann Aubitz for answering my endless questions about how to put this book together.

To my valued insight team:

To the three generations of colleagues and friends who took time out of their busy days to review the various drafts of this book and provide me with valuable feedback to narrow the focus down to the most critical information. Your responses and comments proved these concepts transcend generational divides. Thank you Mary Angela Baker, Morag Barrett, Dawn Bjork, Sharon Gifford and Laura Ledray.

Also Available...

Confidence Plan Workbook

Use this thought-provoking workbook
to develop your own Confidence Plan
based on concepts found in the impactful book
Compounding Your Confidence.

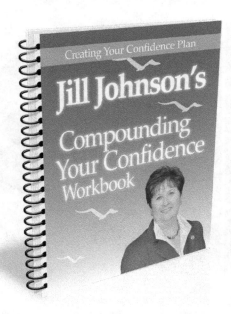

PURCHASE Your Copy NOW!
Bulk discounts available.

www.jcs-usa.com

Also Available...

Recorded Live

Listen to this live recording, of Jill Johnson's
dynamic keynote presentation. You will be transported
into the audience with the 400 other attendees
to learn, laugh and be inspired!

PURCHASE Your Copy NOW!
Bulk discounts available.

www.jcs-usa.com

Johnson
Consulting
Services
Marketing & Management Consultants

Also Available in the BOLD Questions Series...

Business Strategy Edition

52 questions to shape your
business strategies.

PURCHASE Your Copy NOW!
Bulk discounts available.

www.jcs-usa.com

Also Available in the BOLD Questions Series...

Leadership Edition

52 questions to shape your leadership **thinking**.

PURCHASE Your Copy NOW!
Bulk discounts available.

www.jcs-usa.com

Also Available in the BOLD Questions Series...

Decision-Making Edition

52 questions to shape
how you make **decisions.**

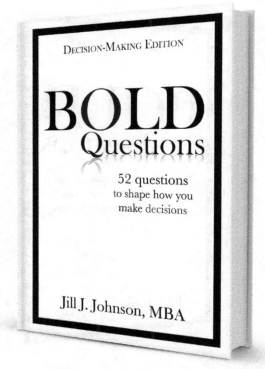